Smith - A Tragic Farce by John Davidson

John Davidson was born at Barrhead, East Renfrewshire on 11th April 1857.

In 1862 his family moved to Greenock and there he began his education at Highlanders' Academy. Davidson would now spend many years at school and the beginnings of a career in various industries before gaining employment in various schools.

By now literature was a large part of his activities and his first published work was 'Bruce, A Chronicle Play' in 1886. Four other plays quickly followed including the somewhat brilliant pantomimic 'Scaramouch in Naxos' (1889).

With his reputation gradually providing an income he was also able to explore his true medium; Verse. 'In a Music Hall and Other Poems' (1891) together with 'Fleet Street Eclogues' (1893) were ample proof that he possessed a quite rare, genuine and distinctive poetic gift.

Davidson now turned further and further towards verse. In 1894 he published his most popular volume, 'Ballads and Songs' (1894), and this was followed by a further 'Fleet Street Eclogues' (Second Series) (1896) and by 'New Ballads' (1897) and 'The Last Ballad' (1899).

As the new century dawned Davidson was hard at work on a series of 'Testaments', in which he gave definite expression to his philosophy and were published over a seven year period; 'The Testament of a Vivisector' (1901), 'The Testament of a Man Forbid' (1901), 'The Testament of an Empire Builder' (1902), and 'The Testament of John Davidson' (1908).

However, on 23rd March 1909, with his finances in ruins, the onset of cancer and profound hopelessness and clinical depression he left his house for the last time. His body was only found on September 18th by some local fishermen.

Index of Contents

I0163559

PERSONS

Smith
Hallowes
Graham
Brown
Jones
Robinson
Two Men-servants
Magdalen
Topsy

SCENE: London and Garth

TIME: The Present

SMITH

ACT I

SCENE:—A Room in a Public-House. Glasses on the Table

BROWN is discovered talking excitedly; **JONES**, attempting to interrupt him; and **ROBINSON**, in a corner with a newspaper.

BROWN
Truth is an airy point between two cliffs
Of adamant opinion: safest he
Who foots it far from either beetling brink.
Hallowes, now: he goes hanging on the verge
His martyr-face and aspirations strung
With bent keys. If his starting eyes behold
Some tartan star, or other fire-flaught born
Of pallid brains ill-nourished on bleached blood,
It is the truth—truth absolute! And down,
Loosing his hold to clasp his fervid hands,
He'll crash, and spill his life on stones untrod.

ROBINSON
Fair—very fair, indeed!

JONES
So would not you!
The Bastille Column or St. Paul's at noon,
Where crowds may see your glossy frock-coat fly,
And wax pathetic o'er the exotic spray
That slips the button-hole in middle air,

And twinkling after, lights upon the mess
Of limbs and oozing blood that late was you.

ROBINSON
Come, let each other be! no answer, Brown;
Because I want to open up a point.
That fellow, Smith—the point is suicide—
He said the other day—why, it was here!—
He would have coffee; we had brandy: well—
You know he speaks to everybody; so,
He cries to Topsy, there, who brought the drink—
He spoils the barmaids with his high-flown talk:
I tried it, and they laughed at me; but he!
He talks philosophy, religion, books:
And they can talk it too, with him. Well, then—

BROWN
Pure innocence: the man's a baby.

JONES
Yes.
Uncultured, too; he lacks the college stamp.

ROBINSON
Well, then, my point—

BROWN
Oh, never mind your point!
You've hit it, Jones; "uncultured" is the word.
Give me a man who knows what language means:
No forging sudden bolts that gild the fact,
A bright enough reality before:
Who never says a thing a thousand ways,
Nibbling with slippery sleight-of-tongue, till chance
Expose the end to bite. Give me a man
Whose mind is ready as a lawyer's desk,
Each pigeon-hole accountable for this,
Each drawer containing that, and nothing else.

JONES
Whose thinking's done; whose automatic mind
Strikes the same absolute response each time.

BROWN
A man who knows the best of everything;
Consummate, bland; whom novelty annoys,
Guessing what musty masquerade it is
Of some dispute of Lamech and his wives.

JONES
Smith's a mere savage, barbarous as a Lapp:
A handsome creature, but elliptical.

BROWN
Something awanting to complete the sense!

ROBINSON
Fair, very fair! But here's a point: you men
Since you began to go about with Smith,
Have caught a little of his style of talk;
You can't deny his power.

BROWN
Power?—seething blood.
Give Jones, or such a man, Smith's body—why,
You'd have the hero of the age! Power? stuff!

JONES
Admit the power—potential as a troop;
But where's the captain?

BROWN
Ay; his brain's a mess
Of sodden sawdust; it ferments and fumes:
But, let me say, wood-spirit's not champagne,
In spite of fables to the contrary.

JONES
Labels, you mean.

ROBINSON
Fair—very fair, by Jove!
Do you go north this year?

BROWN
I do, this week.

ROBINSON
So soon! Health and a happy holiday!

JONES
Your good health and a pleasant time in Garth!

ROBINSON
Here's a point, Brown
Hallowes—he talks of Garth:

I thought the place was only known to you.

BROWN
Hallowes discovered it a year ago:
And there I met him.

JONES
So: I understand
How such an out-at-elbows man as he
Is known to you: there you had no one else.

BROWN
Exactly: with his simple ecstasies
He made good sport when Maudlin took the dumps.

JONES
When do you wed your cousin?

BROWN
In a month.

JONES
Is the day fixed?

BROWN
I go to have it fixed.

ROBINSON
Your cousin, Magdalen ... By Jove, here's Smith!

[Enter **SMITH**.

SMITH
You here! Has Hallowes been?

BROWN
No; not to-night.
Are you to meet him?

SMITH
Yes.

BROWN
He'll not appear:
He acts the people's notion of a poet.
He has a double memorandum-book—
Engagements to be broken—to be kept;
And most of those he makes are for the first:

"Sorry I failed you," when he sees you; "but"—
And you are left to gather that the Muse
Hugged him so close he couldn't get away.

SMITH
He'll not fail me.

JONES
Don't be too sure of that.
I've known him break with me a dozen times.

SMITH
Perhaps he's braver than your other friends.

JONES
The satire's deep.

BROWN
A little underbred—
Hallowes, I mean.

ROBINSON
Still he's a graduate.

JONES
Finished apprentice; but he shuns the stress
Of competition with the journeymen,
Whereby alone dexterity is gained.

BROWN
A fledgling knight who flies the eager fray
Where sword whets sword.

ROBINSON
He herds with nobody,
I've noticed that. But here's a point: I, you,
Smith—everybody wants to know the man;
He—won't be known: no one can equal him
In turning forth the dark slide when you think
Acquaintance burns to intimacy. Smith,
Only you see his lantern blazing bright;
How's that?

BROWN
Speak for yourself, sir. This I know,
He rather courted me. His fitful wisp,
However, I assure you, Robinson,
Leads to a quaking bog of egotism.

JONES
Where I have floundered more than once. A month—
Three weeks ago when he gave up his post
In—Holofernes' School—the Cambridge man's—
That very day I met him here alone.
"I'm done with it," he cried. "These squalid years
Of mental boot-blacking are ended now—
The shameful pedagogy. Ah," he said,
With lips that shook and molten eyes, his voice
Hushing and sparkling as his passion tore
A ragged way through wordy wildernesses,
Or spread, where image failed, in shallows vague,
The margin lost in rushy verbiage,
"Shameful! a devil's compact! I, for food
Have made myself a grindstone, edging souls
Meant most for flying: I, in piteous mouths,
That yearned for sweetest manna, crammed rough stones
And loathsome scorpions: children, youths, the light
Of God brought newly down by love,
Straining to shine on all the flowers of earth,
Of heaven, of poetry, have I swathed up
In noisome fog of the dead letter—I,
Who dare aspire to be a child for ever.
Intolerance in religion never dreamt
Such fell machinery of Acts and Codes
As now we use for nipping thought in bud,
And turning children out like nine-pins, each
As doleful and as wooden. Never more
Shall I put hand to such inhuman work!"
To come with this to me, who teach, and mean
To start a boarding-school next year!

BROWN
By Jove!
The net result of solitude. This world,
This oyster with its valves of toil and play,
Would round his corners for its own good ease,
And make a pearl of him if he'd plunge in.

SMITH
Then you would change the diamonds into pearls,
The rubies and the opals?

ROBINSON
Very fair!

BROWN

Better a pure pearl than a damaged diamond.

JONES
And in this matter we may all be pearls.

SMITH
Be worldlings, truly. I would rather be
A shred of glass that sparkles in the sun,
And keeps a lowly rainbow of its own,
Than one of those so trim and patent pearls
With hearts of sand veneered, sewed up and down
The stiff brocade society affects.

ROBINSON
Fair, very fair!

JONES
Be quiet, parroquet!
Are we such pearls?

SMITH
Pearls! This is what you are:
The commonest type of biped crawling here.
Take it thus crudely: you would not believe
A subtle phrase in full, but think I meant
Less than the words might bear, deeming me dull—
Barbarian you call me ...

BROWN
Who said that?

SMITH
The friends of gossips gossip, little Brown.

BROWN
The great Smith gossips too, then.

SMITH
What! You fool!
You dare to bandy words with me! Begone!
Get out of here the three of you!

JONES
He's mad.

SMITH
You sots, you maggots, shavings, asteroids!
A million of you wouldn't make a man!

Out, or I'll strike you, monkeys, mannikins!

[**ALL** go out; then re-enter **SMITH**, followed by **TOPSY** with salver, etc.

SMITH
You're looking fresh: You've had a holiday?

TOPSY
I've had my week.

SMITH
Where were you?

TOPSY
At the coast.

SMITH
Now, tell me, what of all you saw, remains?

TOPSY
Oh, well—there's many a thing! There's—
Ah! there's this! One morning early that I stood alone,
And saw the green sea from a windy cliff,
With small, white, curling waves, like shavings pinned
Upon a watered silk.

SMITH
Oh! how was that?

TOPSY
There was a great Scotch lady long ago—
I read it in a penny paper there;
That made me think of it; and she was poor,
And wore, instead of ribbons, shavings once,
And was the belle and made a match that night.
Here's Mr. Hallowes, sir.

SMITH
The same for him.

[Enter **HALLOWES**.

[**TOPSY** goes out, and returns as before, and goes out again.

HALLOWES
Smith, I congratulate you. Come, your hand.

SMITH

Thank you; I'm very pleased indeed. On what?

HALLOWES
On the great gladness you're about to feel.
I've lost my post—dismissed—incompetence.

SMITH
So soon! I said three months: it's just three weeks.
Business is worse than teaching, then.

HALLOWES
Oh, worse!
Give me a week to coin its condemnation!
Business—the world's work—is the sale of lies:
Not goods, but trade-marks; and still more and more
In every branch becomes the sale of money:
Why, goods are now the means of bartering gold!

SMITH
It fits these reeling times of tail-wagged dogs.

HALLOWES
But wish me joy.

SMITH
Joy, friend, till pain be ease!

HALLOWES
Now will I tell you what I mean to do.
Garth's in the North, a hamlet like a cave,
Nestling unknown in tawny Merlin's side,
A mount, brindled with scars and waterways.
The windows, Argus-eyed with knotted panes
That under heavy brows of roses blink
Blind guard, have never wept with hailstones stung;
No antique, gnarled, and wrinkled, roundwood porch,
Whiskered with hollyhocks in this old thorpe
Has ever felt the razor of the East:
No rail, no coach, no tourist passes there:
But in the brooding evening from her seat,
A worn tree-trunk, the toothless beldame leaps
As lithe as superstition, says a saw,
And kills the toad that in the channel hops;
Far up the mountain children's voices ring;
The quoiters cry; and past the ivied inn
A chastened brook tells all its pebbled beads;
Between the bourtrie-bushes and the thorns
The commonest bird that sings is wonderful,

So empty are the spaces of the air
From any breath of modern weariness.
There will I live and walk the mountain-side,
Looking across the strath upon a stream,
A beakerful of water, spilt along
A winding strip of green and bosky spray,
That showers in silver when light-fingered winds
Turn up the leaves: a ridge, fire-reared and low,
Of coppice-covered hills, scalloped against
A loftier mass of purple, nobly borne,
Gives body to the sunset: night and day,
Asleep or waking, earth in heaven's lap lies.

SMITH
And is this to be wholly holiday?

HALLOWES
I shall make poetry—a line a day,
If nothing more. I'm twenty: I may count
On ten years yet. Three thousand lines, each line
A very mountain from whose sun-gilt crest
The stormy world a peaceful picture seems.
I shall upheave and range a chain like this:
Realms shall rejoice in it: my fame shall grow
For ever like the sward.

SMITH
Let fame alone.

HALLOWES
You misconceive: fame is the breath of power:
What valid work was ever for itself
Wrought solely, be it war, art, statesmanship?
Nothing can be its own reward and hold
Rank above patience, or whatever game,
Angling or avarice, is selfisher.
O watering palates! and, O skyey grapes!
O purple path above the milky way!
Give me to dream dreams all would love to dream;
To tell the world's truth; hear the world tramp time
With satin slippers and with hob-nailed shoes
To my true singing: fame is worth its cost,
Blood-sweats, and tears, and haggard, homeless lives.
How dare a man, appealing to the world,
Content himself with ten! How dare a man
Appeal to ten when all the world should hear!
How dare a man conceive himself as else
Than his own fool without the world's hurrah

To echo him!

SMITH
But if the world won't shout
Till he be dead?

HALLOWES
Let him address the street:
No subtle essences, ethereal tones
For senses sick, bed-ridden in the down
Of culture and its stifling curtains. Gusts
From bean-fields and the pine-woods, thought and deed
Of the young world bursting its swaddling bands
Before the upturned eyes and warning palms
Of fangless Use and Wont, his nurses hoar—
These find an echo everywhere.

SMITH
The world
Still follows culture, though.

HALLOWES
Maybe. But it
Follows itself, and shall, Narcissus-like,
Perish of self-love.

SMITH
Echo, what of her?

HALLOWES
She shall be re-incarnate by the word
That she shall hear.

SMITH
What word?

HALLOWES
It is not said.

SMITH
Who shall pronounce it?

HALLOWES
Who knows?—You, or I?

SMITH
Well said! We'll go together to the North.

HALLOWES
What! are you free?

SMITH
I am. You want to write:
I want to think. When shall we start?

HALLOWES
To-morrow.

SMITH
So soon! But you are right: one must become
Fanatic—be a wedge—a thunder-bolt,
To smite a passage through the close-grained world.

[They go out.

ACT II

SCENE:—An Arbour in Graham's Orchard

Enter **SMITH**, **HALLOWES**, and **GRAHAM**.

GRAHAM
Now, rest you here; I've business in the house:
And when I come I'll bring my daughter. Ha!
[To **HALLOWES**]
She lives on poetry; you'll soon be friends;
[To **SMITH**]
While you and I and Brown will talk again
Of London. What!—you called it—let me see—
The running sore, the ringworm of the earth.
Good, very good.

[Goes out.

HALLOWES
You'll make excuse for me.

SMITH
Why are you so reluctant to remain?

HALLOWES
You do not see the meaning of the knight.
We trespass in his wood: he meets us; storms,
And plays his gamekeeper. Our witty talk

Changes his character, and—we are here:
But mark, on trial; else, not his arbour,
But his drawing-room.

SMITH
He brings his daughter, though.

HALLOWES
True; but you see our humour was so broad.

SMITH
Therefore he does not take us to his house?
Suppose it so, is he the less a man?
Why, it's a powerful thing to do.

HALLOWES
Indeed!
Snobbish, say I.

SMITH
Away, man! Use that word!
A poet, too! Oh, I could rail at it! Snob!
It's a modern word; and so is cad:
None use them but deservers of them. Faugh;
So bitterly I hate them, into sense
My spleen spins slovenly. We all are men.
Doomsday of nicknames! I behold it dawn.
An inky cloud, with thick corrosive stench,
Blots out the heavens, and like a palimpsest
Shows name on name in smoking characters,
A leprous scroll, too filthy to o'er-read:
Beneath them, branded deep athwart the cloud
In letters huge from which the light scales off,
The most inhuman, most ungodly word,
Sinner. But lo! the rotten-fuming signs
Smoulder and writhe, and run like mercury,
Flooding the cloud, which belches into flame
And shrivels up beyond the bounds of space!
A rose-dipped pencil washes suddenly
A blush along the east, whereon appears
In molten gold, Man, Woman; and I know
That we are all one race, and these nicknames,
Phantasmal charnel-lights of self-contempt.

HALLOWES
You know I have not always strength of wing
To soar like you right to God's point of view.
Pardon the word. Now, you must let me go.

SMITH
You give no cause: poetic mood won't do.
I see a mental sickness in your eye:
What is it, Hallowes?

HALLOWES
Why, my money's done:
And day by day from London packets come—
Dramas and poems, essays and reviews,
Returned with thanks, returned with thanks.

SMITH
Just so.
Ten pounds I have: take half: when this is spent
Then we return with thanks to London town.
You have your ticket?

HALLOWES
Oh, yes!

SMITH
Cheer up, then!
We have a fortnight yet. Sit down and talk
Of comfortable things. We'll meditate
Upon return-tickets for a while:
How beautifully suited to our need,
Spendthrifts like us! Devise some praise for them.

HALLOWES
O let me go! I have my note-book here.
I'll climb to Merlin-top and write all night
Under the moon or till you follow me.

SMITH
Away then, since you must! Good luck, good rhymes!

[**HALLOWES** goes out. Enter **MAGDALEN** without seeing **SMITH**.

[Aside]
These plaited coils of hair, the golden lid
Of the rich casket where her live thoughts lie:
Her cheek is tinged with sunset? Has she eyes?
Her body sways: the crimson-blazoned west
Like organ-music surges through her blood.
My seeming aimless visit to the North—
The time—the circumstance!—I yield myself!
This is the woman whom my soul will love.

She moves this way, backward, to sit. I'll speak.
Lady.

[**MAGDALEN** wheels round.

Her eyes are living sapphires!

MAGDALEN
What!

SMITH
I love you.

MAGDALEN
Sir!

SMITH
I love you, lady.

MAGDALEN [About to go]
Sir!

SMITH
Lady, stay.
My body and my soul assembled here,
At war till now, are wedded by your glance:
You make that man which chaos was before:
And this is love. I dreaded love: I knew
It should with such a pang lay hold of me.
I am not mad although I tremble thus:
It is the inspiration of my love.
Fly not, repulse me not, and do not fear:
I would tear up my body with my hands,
And hide you in my heart did evil threat:
I am as tame to you as wild things are
To those that cherish them. Be confident,
For I shall guard my dreams from harming you
As faithfully as time his vigil keeps.

MAGDALEN
I do not fear.

SMITH
Speak louder, speak again.
Like rose-leaves that enrich the greedy earth
The tremulous whispering bedews my heart.
Speak, speak!

MAGDALEN

Who are you, sir?

SMITH

A mellow voice,
Falling like thistledown, melting like snow,
Golden and searching as a sunny wine.
It bore a question: Who am I? A man.
Magdalen [aside]. I think so too.—What do you want with me?

SMITH

Our language is too worn, too much abused,
Jaded and over-spurred, wind-broken, lame,—
The hackneyed roadster every bagman mounts.
I cannot tell you what I want with you,
Unless you understand the depth of this:
I want for you heroic happiness.

MAGDALEN

How might I win this happiness?

SMITH

Be mine:
I am the enemy of all the world:
Dare it with me: be mine.

MAGDALEN

I know you not.
I am engaged to one I do not love;
My father swears that I must marry him:
It is a common misery, so stale
That I contemned it: and I know you not:
But I have courage. Let me think a while.

SMITH

Think my thought; be impatient as I am;
Obey your nature, not authority:
Because the world, enchanted by the sun,
The moon, the stars, with charms of time and space,
Of seasons, tides, of darkness and of light,
Weaves new enchantment everlastingly,
Whirled in a double spell of day and year,
A self-deluded sorcerer, winding round,
Close to its smothered heart, coil after coil
Of magic zones, invisible as air—
Some, Cytherean belts; some, chains; and some,
Noisome and terrible as hooded snakes.

MAGDALEN
What do you mean? what spells? what sorcery?

SMITH
The hydra-headed creeds; the sciences,
That deem the thing is known when it is named;
And literature, thought's palace-prison fair;
Philosophy, the grand inquisitor
That racks ideas and is fooled with lies;
Society, the mud wherein we stand
Up to the eyes, whence if I drag you forth,
Saving your soul and mine, there shall ascend
A poisonous blast that may o'ertake our lives.

MAGDALEN
I feel a meaning in your eloquence;
I see my poor thoughts made celestial
Like faded women Jove hung in the sky.
Obey my nature, sir? How shall I know
The voice of nature from the thousand cries,
That clamour in my head like piteous birds,
Filling the air about a lonely isle
With ringing terror when the hunter comes.

SMITH
Shut out the storm and heed the still, small voice.

MAGDALEN
Have pity. Yet I think the woman's dream
Is given me—the strong deliverer
To pluck her from the dragon's jaws unharmed.
What can I say? Rest still your eyes on mine,
And I shall dare to speak. I love you, sir;
And I have loved you since I was a girl—
You, only you. Good-bye. Oh, in my life—
A miracle, I think, as this world goes—
I met the living image of my dream,
And was found worthy to be loved! Good-bye.
I seem to see my daughter at my knees,
Listening with violet eyes of heaven-wide awe,
The virgin story I shall utter once
To her, only to her.

SMITH
And so, you go
To hell.

MAGDALEN

Ay, even so: my father's word
Is plighted to this man, and so is mine.
Perhaps, that I may know this is no dream—
Sir, will you kiss me?

[He folds her in his arms and kisses her.

SMITH
You are faint, my love.

MAGDALEN
Oh, have pity, sir!

SMITH
I will have pity.

[Goes out carrying her. Then enter **BROWN**. He goes out after them, and re-enters running as the curtain falls.

ACT III

SCENE.—The Top of Mount Merlin: A Precipice on One Side: Rocks on the Other

HALLOWES is discovered lying with a note-book by his side.

HALLOWES
O noblest hour in my ignoble life!
Hunger and squalor, and delirious rhymes;
No past, no future; one unending now
Of meanest misery, most miserable
When fairest dreams gilded the starless night,
And words in choirs flew singing through my brain
Melodious thunder, for then most I knew
The yawning wants and gnawing cares of life.
To sink to that inanity abhorred,
The wretch whose early fervour, burnt away,
Leaves him, for lack of ease to smite his thought
To white-heat—since the brazier of youth,
That needs no sweat, is cold—incapable
Of any meaning, but with loathsome itch
That still essays, and still produces nought,
Or horribly emits untempered scraps—
Toads, cinders, snakes, nameless aborted things,—
The hideous castings witchcraft vomited;
Maybe to live on grudging charity
Of friends estranged; sneered at by smug success;

Called poetaster: such had been my life;
But I have chosen death. Death—and the moon
Hangs low and broad upon the eastern verge
Above a mist that floods the orient,
Filling the deep ravines and shallow vales,
Lake-like and wan, embossed with crested isles
Of pine and birch. Death—and the drops of day
Still stain the west a faintest tinge of rose
The stars cannot o'erwash with innocence.
Death—and the mountain-tops, peak after peak,
Lie close and dark beneath Orion's sword.
Death—and the houses nestle at my feet,
With ruddy human windows here and there
Piercing the velvet shade—deep in the world,
Old hedge-rows and sweet by-paths through the corn!
The river like a sleepless eye looks up.
Pale shafts of smoke ascend from homely hearths,
And fade in middle air like happy sighs.
Death—and the wind blows chill across my face:
The thin, long, hoary grass waves at my side
With muffled tinkling.... Not yet! No; my life
Has not ebbed all away: I want to live
A little while.... Is the moon gone so soon?
They've put the shutters to, down there.... The wind
Is warm.... Death—is it death? ... I had no chance....
Perhaps I'll have another where I go....
Another chance.... How black!...

[Dies.

[Enter **SMITH** carrying **MAGDALEN**.

MAGDALEN
I think now I can walk again.

SMITH
No need;
We've reached the summit: see, the circling world!
Does this seem madness still?

MAGDALEN
Mad happiness:
I know we should be here. Ah! there's a man!

SMITH
My friend, the poet. He has chosen well:
The cream-white moon, this high peak of the earth—
The earth, itself the one Parnassus-mount.

MAGDALEN

And have you climbed the hill only for him
Bearing me half the way? But answer not:
I only wish to feel that I am yours;
And that this knowledge may be fully mine,
Call me my name. You do not know my name?

SMITH

And wish not: you are woman; I am man.
Why should we limit all the thought of this,
Shrouding the Infinite with names? Our life
Is haunted by these ghosts ourselves have raised.
O lady, we shall never know the truth,
What man, what love, what God is, till we cease
To talk of them—which all do in the grave.

MAGDALEN

How strange it seems to me and yet not strange:
Death, life, I care not which, so I am yours.

SMITH

And I yours, now, for ever.—Hallowes!—What!—
Asleep?—pale ... dead! ... This was a man too slight,
Too sweet to live. I think he has done well:
For had he stayed strung naked on life's wheel,
Broken by every circumstance of woe,
He had gone mad. This sight would pierce my heart,
But that yours bucklers mine. A girl-like boy!
He used to talk of euthanasia:
How has he killed himself? Here's blood! He said
That should he ever need to take his life
Thus gently would he ope a sluice and die.
I loved him. I shall weep some other time.
What has he written here?

[While **SMITH** examines the note-book enter **GRAHAM**, **BROWN**, and **TWO MEN-SERVANTS**. Scored and
re-scored,—Illegible.

MAGDALEN

Oh!—my father!

GRAHAM

So, sir!
What Jupiter are you that walk away
With ladies over mountains in the night!
What radiant devil rather! With an art,
Seven times refining the seducer's dross,

You brand the reputation curelessly.
And leave the spotless sufferer to pine,
The guiltless-guilty in a hell of woe.
Or are you but a thundering, blundering fool,
Mad, not malignant? Do you understand?
to-morrow all the county shall declare,
And shortly London echo how Graham's girl—
Graham, the old fool, who never stirred from Garth,
And out of harm's way kept his daughter snug,
Filtering her reading, her acquaintanceship—
Never a man but Brown, her lord to be—
How she, when he, too confident because
She just had named the day, brought home that night—
The first time since his daughter turned fifteen—
Two men, wild London fellows—hark, away,
With both among the heather, o'er the moor!
For there's your friend, I see, sir. Do you see?
What's to do? Who is to suffer? Speak, sir!
Maudlin, he stares at you; you, at the ground—
But that is well, Brown, speak to him—to them.

BROWN
Love holds my tongue, sir.

GRAHAM
What! do you love him?
Why, now, as we came panting up the hill,
You swore he was a mean adventurer,
Poor as a rat, and friendless as a toad:
A scribbling, bibbling, fribbling, poet, he
Who takes it all so coolly there.

SMITH
He's dead.

GRAHAM
Dead!—O my God!—my head—my heart is split:
No hiding now. O man, man, you have done
Worse than you think! In every ha'penny rag,
Cried in the streets, the talk of billiard-rooms—
My daughter Magdalen!—my happiness,
My poem, picture, my divinity!
I haven't fired a gun, or touched a card,
Donned buckskin, made a bet, for five long years.
I've led a dog's life; done dog's duty too;
And been as happy as a faithful dog:
And all to save my daughter from the taint
That taints me, taints the world, and taints the best:

I've no fine names for it; I know it's there.
I've taught her everything—professors, books:
Made her a—what's the word?—a paragon:
And now I've got my nephew here, young Brown,
Who had a grandfather, who had one too—
An Oxford man, a wholesome, handsome boy,
Rich, well-disposed, to marry her: and here,
Safe in my pocket, is their honeymoon—
A map, I mean, where I will follow them—
I've marked in red the route they'll take, you see—
Before I go to bed. I'll have my fling
After they're married—do you understand?
My poem out, my picture on the line,
I'll dance, and sing, and dine, and wine, and shine!
My God, Magdalen, don't stand staring there!
The moon can't help you, bouncing as it is.
I'm going mad. Brown, take my daughter home.

MAGDALEN
Father I cannot, now, go home to-night,
Unless he comes with us.

GRAHAM
He! whom? What! him?

MAGDALEN
Father, for him you sacrificed yourself,
Not knowing how you wrought on fate's behalf.
Most loving and most noble father, thanks:
My heart is aching with deep thankfulness.
Never had daughter such a holy time
Of preparation: any other life
Would not have made me meet for him.

GRAHAM
Girl! girl!
Be quiet, now!—Brown, tell us what to do!

BROWN
Keep cool, as I am. Smith, I know your power:
You are the kind of man that healthy girls
Yield to at once, you know.

GRAHAM
What's this? What's this?
You've lost your head, I think.

MAGDALEN

O father, look!
See with my eyes. He's worth a million Browns.—
[To **BROWN**]
Sir, pardon me. You are a worthy man,
And much above the common stamp, I know.
Father, this man—I do not know his name—
Is all the world to me.

GRAHAM
You little fool!

[He hands **MAGDALEN** over to **BROWN** and the **SERVANTS**.

Now, sir, I'll pay you down a thousand pounds
To keep this quiet.... Oh, the murdered man!
Ay; he's been murdered: here's the murderer:
That's the way out of it! Ha, ha! my buck,
We'll have you clapped in jail.

BROWN
That wouldn't do.
I'll add another thousand. Keep our names ...

SMITH
Magdalen!

MAGDALEN
Yours, only yours.

GRAHAM
Be quiet!
What's to be done? See you here, ravisher—
But stop a bit: we're all assuming. Brown,
Perhaps there is some satisfactory—
Some explanation, plausible at least.
Sir, have you anything to say?

SMITH
Much. First:
You are my enemy, and I am yours.
Rancorous debates, and wars, and martyrdoms
Give tolerance the most forlorn of hopes;
But with the impartial moon for ensign, here
I dare assay to make my foe my friend.
Even one who overlooked the world with me,
And saw it, as I see it, a flying shuttle,
Weaving a useless web of mystery
That shrouds itself—even he, whose piteous blood

Stains this green mountain-brow the soft clouds kiss,
And sweet wild winds freshen continually,
Had not discerned the reason of our deed:
How much less you, who never think at all!
But you must listen: you must try to think.
And see how simple is our presence here:
The way to town is five miles by the road,
And two across the hill; so this I chose,
Being shorter, and because my friend had said
He would await my coming. She and I
Are on our way to London.

GRAHAM
You are mad:
You've made her mad. Good-night.

[He is about to lead **MAGDALEN** away but **SMITH** holds him.

SMITH
Not so: We are not mad, but you—the world is mad.
You and the world would make her such a thing
As poets still cry out on. Mine she is,
Mine by the love that, as we had been gods
Meeting in golden Tempe, dawned and shone
Full-beamed at once. What is more sane than love?
The universe is chaos without love....

GRAHAM
Hold off!

SMITH
Be still!—Women are made by men:
The nations fade that hold their women slaves:
The souls of men that pave their hell-ward path
With women's souls lose immortality.
What station in our heart's economy—
The hidden household where our naked thoughts
Stand at the windows innocent as babes,
Or crouch in corners shamefaced and undone,
Though none may pass but he whose thoughts they are:
What home, or what foul den we keep them in,
These complements of us, these plastic things
Our fancy fashions to the shape we please—
That is the test of sanity. Behold,
Your daughter, being throned within my heart,
Has straight become a queen!

GRAHAM

What noise is that?

SMITH
A cry within the wind. Have you ne'er heard
Prophetic voices muffled in the blast?
Old man, you've done a high thing for your child;
But all is naught if you constrain her now.
Give me the woman whom my soul has chosen,
Give me the woman who has chosen me.

GRAHAM
Poor fool! no frantic whim will change my plan.

[**GRAHAM** and **BROWN** lead **MAGDALEN** out. **SMITH** attempts to take her from them but the **SERVANTS** interfere. He hurls them both to the ground: they rise and run out. **SMITH** goes out, and re-enters backward with **MAGDALEN** on one arm, keeping **GRAHAM** and **BROWN** off with the other. He stops at the edge of the cliff.

SMITH
Back, or we plunge together.

GRAHAM
Hold!
[Aside]
That sound!
How could they know? But yet, they saw us go.
It is the village coming up the hill!
They'll rescue us. Brown, we must seem to yield.
This is a madman, no idealist.

BROWN
Stark, staring mad.

GRAHAM
Of course. We might have known.
Why, I could laugh. Come on, we'll humour him.—
Conclusions reached with salience, sir, are oft
Wiser than those we plod to; for the mind
Tires on the dusty round-about; and so
I think you have deserved my daughter.

SMITH
Ha!
Then you are but a worldling after all:
I know your thought: I've met it face to face
A hundred times; and though it owns it not,
It means that all it cannot understand
Is madness, and that highest God is mad.

Is it because the moon is in a cloud
You speak this folly now?—a human voice!
Some people on the hill! I see your drift.—
Magdalen Graham ...

MAGDALEN
Yours, always, only yours.

BROWN
I warn you, monstrous rogue, abduction earns
A lengthy term of penal servitude.

SMITH
Inept fool!—Lady, life, the shooting star,
Is no more worth than is the miser's gold,
The cultured man's impressions, lust's delight;
It is a prison innocence may break;
A moment mere of immortality.

MAGDALEN
Watch for the moon: she slips her sable shawl,
And silver lace. Behold!

SMITH
The happy night
Heaves a deep long-drawn sigh of sweet content.

MAGDALEN
Oh, if the world would look on us like that!

SMITH
The world for you and me is one blank stare—
A basilisk would shrivel up our souls.

MAGDALEN
O these hoarse shouts and fiendish empty shrieks!
How near the people are! Can we not go?

SMITH
Yes, we can go where none will follow us.
We two could never love each other more
Than now we do; never our souls could mount
Higher on passion's fire-plumed wings; nor yet
Could laughter of our children's children pierce
With keener pangs of happiness our hearts.
I have a million things to tell my love,
But I will keep them for eternity.
Good earth, good mother earth, my mate and me—

Take us.

[He leaps with her over the precipice. **GRAHAM** rushes forward, but falls fainting. Enter **VILLAGERS**, shouting and laughing.

John Davidson – A Short Biography

John Davidson was born at Barrhead, East Renfrewshire on 11th April 1857, the son of Alexander Davidson, an Evangelical Union minister and Helen née Crocket of Elgin.

In 1862 the family moved to Greenock and Davidson began his education at Highlanders' Academy. From there he began his career, aged a mere 13, at the chemical laboratory of Walker's Sugarhouse refinery. A year later he returned to Highlander's, this time as a pupil teacher.

During his later employment at the Public Analysts' Office, 1870–71 he developed a keen interest in science which later became an important characteristic of his poetry. He returned once again to the Highlander's Academy, this time for four years, in 1872, again as a pupil teacher. In 1876 he spent a year at Edinburgh University before his first scholastic employment at Alexander's Charity, Glasgow which led to short periods of employment at various other schools over the following half a dozen years.

This led to a stint at Morrison's Academy in Crieff (1885–88), and in a private school at Greenock (1888–89).

In 1885 Davidson married Margaret McArthur and the marriage produced two children, Alexander (born in 1887) and Menzies (born in 1889).

Davidson's first published work was 'Bruce, A Chronicle Play', written in the Elizabethan style, and published by a local Glasgow imprint in 1886. Four other plays quickly followed; 'Smith, A Tragic Farce' (1888), 'An Unhistorical Pastoral' (1889), 'A Romantic Farce' (1889), and then the somewhat brilliant pantomime 'Scaramouch in Naxos' (1889).

By now he was very much immersed in literature and, in 1889, he ventured to London where he frequented the famous Fleet Street pub 'Ye Olde Cheshire Cheese' and joined the 'Rhymers' Club', a poets group that was based there.

Davidson was a prolific and hard-working writer. As well as his plays he wrote for the Speaker, the Glasgow Herald, and several other papers. He also wrote and had published several novels and tales, with perhaps the best being 'Perfervid' (1890).

With his reputation gradually providing an income he was also able to explore his true medium; Verse. 'In a Music Hall and Other Poems' (1891) together with 'Fleet Street Eclogues' (1893) were ample proof that he possessed a quite rare, genuine and distinctive poetic gift. Praise came from his peers including George Gissing and WB Yeats who wrote that it was: 'An example of a new writer seeking out new subject matter, new emotions'.

Davidson now turned further and further towards verse. In 1894 he published his most popular volume, 'Ballads and Songs' (1894), and this was followed by a further 'Fleet Street Eclogues' (Second Series) (1896) and by 'New Ballads' (1897) and 'The Last Ballad' (1899).

Davidson was a prolific writer. Besides the works cited, he wrote many other works including, 'The Wonderful Mission of Earl Lavender' (1895), a novel which extends his literary canon to flagellation erotica. He also contributed an introduction to Shakespeare's Sonnets (Renaissance edition, 1908), which, like his various prefaces and essays, shows him to be a subtle literary critic.

As the new century dawned Davidson was hard at work on a series of 'Testaments', in which he gave definite expression to his philosophy and these were published over a seven year period; 'The Testament of a Vivisector' (1901), 'The Testament of a Man Forbid' (1901), 'The Testament of an Empire Builder' (1902), and 'The Testament of John Davidson' (1908).

Though he played down any thought of himself as a philosopher, he expounded an original philosophy which was at once materialistic and aristocratic.

His later verse, which is often fine rhetoric rather than poetry, expressed his belief which is summed up in the last words that he wrote, "Men are the universe become conscious; the simplest man should consider himself too great to be called after any name." Davidson professed to reject all existing philosophies, including that of Nietzsche, as inadequate. The poet planned to expand and expound on his revolutionary creed in a trilogy entitled 'God and Mammon'. Only two plays, however, were written, 'The Triumph of Mammon' (1907) and 'Mammon and his Message' (1908).

In addition to his own work Davidson was a noted translator of other works which included Montesquieu's 'Lettres Persanes' (1892), François Coppée's 'Pour la Couronne' in 1896 and Victor Hugo's 'Ruy Blas' in 1904, the former being produced as, 'For the Crown', at the Lyceum Theatre in 1896, the latter as 'A Queen's Romance' at the Imperial Theatre.

Frank Harris, a member of the Rhymers' Club and himself a writer of erotic literature described him in 1889 as: "... a little below middle height, but strongly built with square shoulders and remarkably fine face and head; the features were almost classically regular, the eyes dark brown and large, the forehead high, the hair and moustache black. His manners were perfectly frank and natural; he met everyone in the same unaffected kindly human way; I never saw a trace in him of snobbishness or incivility. Possibly a great man, I said to myself, certainly a man of genius, for simplicity of manner alone is in England almost a proof of extraordinary endowment."

In 1906 he was awarded a civil list pension of £100 per annum and George Bernard Shaw did what he could to help him financially. However other issues were also circling besides poverty. Ill-health, and his declining intellectual powers, amplified by the onset of cancer, caused profound hopelessness and clinical depression.

Late in 1908, Davidson left London to live in Penzance in Cornwall. On 23rd March 1909, he left his house and was not seen again. There seemed no sound reason not to believe that he had done so with the intention of drowning himself. On an examination of his office a new manuscript was found. It was a poetry book; 'Fleet Street Poems', with a letter bleakly stating confirming, "This will be my last book."

Indeed in his philosophic book 'The Testament of John Davidson', published the year before his death, he anticipates this fate:

"None should outlive his power. . . . Who kills
Himself subdues the conqueror of kings;
Exempt from death is he who takes his life;
My time has come."

Davidson's body was not discovered until 18th September in Mount's cave by some fishermen. In accordance with his will it was now buried at sea. Strangely it seemed Davidson's wish that none of his unpublished works, nor any biography be published and "no word except of my writing is ever to appear in any book of mine as long as the copyright endures."

Davidson's poetry was a key early influence on important Modernist poets, in particular, his compatriot Hugh MacDiarmid, Wallace Stevens and T.S. Eliot.

John Davidson – A Concise Bibliography

The North Wall (1885)
Diabolus Amans (1885) Verse drama
Bruce (1886) A drama in five acts
Smith (1888) A tragedy
An Unhistorical Pastoral, A Romantic Farce (1889)
Scaramouch in Naxos (1889)
Perfervid: The Career of Ninian Jamieson (1890) with 23 Original Illustrations by Harry Furniss
The Great Men, And a Practical Novelist (1891) Illustrated by E. J. Ellis.
In a Music Hall, and other Poems (1891)
Laura Ruthven's Widowhood (with C. J. Wills) (1892)
Fleet Street Eclogues (1893)
The Knight of the Maypole, (1903)
Sentences and Paragraphs (1893)
Ballads and Songs (1894)
Baptist Lake (1894)
A Random Itinerary (1894)
A Full and True Account of the Wonderful Mission of Earl Lavender (1895)
St. George's Day (1895)
Fleet Street Eclogues (Second Series) (1896)
Miss Armstrong's and Other Circumstances (1896)
The Pilgrimage of Strongsoul and Other Stories (1896)
New Ballads (1897)
Godfrida, a play (1898)
The Last Ballad (1899)
Self's the Man, A tragi-comedy (1901)
The Testament of a Man Forbid (1901)
The Testament of a Vivisector (1901)
The Testament of an Empire Builder (1902)

A Rosary (1903)
The Knight of the Maypole: A Comedy in Four Acts (1903)
The Testament of a Prime Minister (1904)
The Ballad of a Nun (1905)
The Theatrocrat: A Tragic Play of Church and State (1905)
Holiday and other poems, with a note on poetry (1906)
The Triumph of Mammon (1907)
Mammon and His Message (1908)
The Testament of John Davidson (1908)
Fleet Street and other Poems (1909)

He was also a contributor to 'The Yellow Book' periodical

As Translator

Montesquieu's Lettres Persanes (Persian Letters) (1892)
François Coppée's Pour la couronne (For the Crown) (1896)
Victor Hugo's Ruy Blas (A Queen's Romance) (1904)